Piano Solo

DAVID LANZ
Liverpool
Re-Imagining the Beatles

ISBN 978-1-61774-037-4

7777 W. BLUEMOUND RD. P.O. BOX 13819 MILWAUKEE, WI 53213

Visit Hal Leonard Online at
www.halleonard.com

Liverpool

Liverpool, England . . . a city on the banks of the Mersey River (The river made famous in the 1964 hit song *Ferry Across The Mersey* by Gerry and the Pacemakers, and found in my *Songs From An English Garden* songbook).

Liverpool, the birthplace of John, Paul, George, and Ringo, and where we begin our musical journey.

The title track was composed as a tribute, an emotional overture of sorts, imbued with subtle musical phrasing from The Fab Four. From here, we traverse through a decade of Lennon and McCartney songs, arranged and re-imagined through the lens of my own musical voice, which admittedly, has been joyfully shaped and informed by this great and enduring legacy of musical history - a time so explosive and fruitful we may never see anything like it again.

I spent nearly half a year listening, selecting and arranging this material before entering the studio. Once the lion's share of the recording was complete, my friend and collaborator, Gary Stroutsos, who can be heard on flute on the *Liverpool* recording , along with photographer and personal assistant, Carole May, took off on a pilgrimage to Liverpool, England, to see where the music of the Beatles all began.

Shortly after our arrival, we were given an extraordinary tour by England's National Trust. It started with an intimate inside look at John Lennon's boyhood home where he lived from the age of five until he was twenty-three.

I was completely taken off guard at the impact the spirit of place had on me. This was especially true when I climbed the stairs and stood by myself in the small bedroom that had been John's, the room where he had done much of his early imaginative dreaming. Chills ran through me and ghosts from the past were palpable.

It was here in this house named Mendips that 14-year-old Paul McCartney and 17-year-old John Lennon began their friendship and started a song writing partnership that would change the world.

They also soon began meeting and writing songs in Paul McCartney's more modest home, less than a mile away from Mendips, at 20 Forthlin Road.

Our tour continued through the McCartney home. One of the outstanding features was the black and white original photographs taken by Paul's younger brother, Michael. Photos capturing family, friends, and everyday household events. Most notable was a photograph of the two teenage musicians, sitting in Paul's small living room, holding guitars, notebook opened to the hand written lyrics of an early Lennon and McCartney classic, *I Saw Her Standing There*.

I am so grateful for the chance to have connected in such an intimate way and to have come full circle with two of my greatest musical role models.

I will never forget the time spent in Liverpool: the drive down Penny Lane, standing by the gate at Strawberry Field . . . all giving new meaning and greater dimension to the music of the Beatles.

"There are places I remember . . . All my life . . ."

David Lanz

DAVID LANZ
Liverpool
Re-Imagining the Beatles

LIVERPOOL

By DAVID LANZ

Expressively

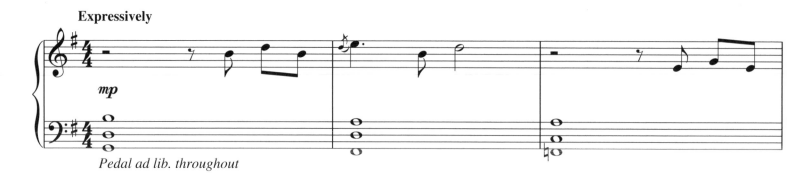

Pedal ad lib. throughout

Moderately, steadily

a tempo

rit.

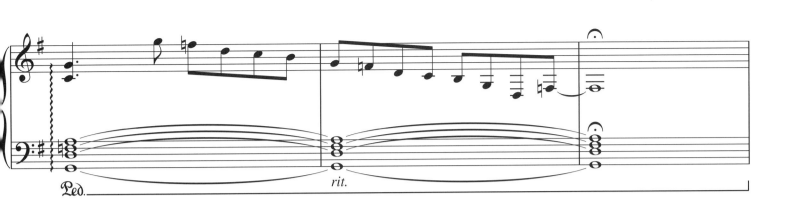

Freely

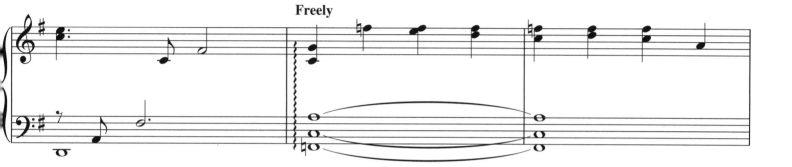

THINGS WE SAID TODAY

Words and Music by JOHN LENNON
and PUAL McCARTNEY

Slowly, very freely

(Guitar transcribed for piano)

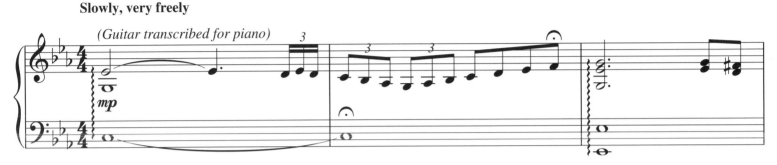

Moderately, steadily
(Piano as recorded)

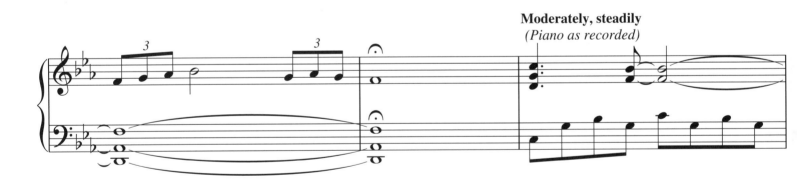

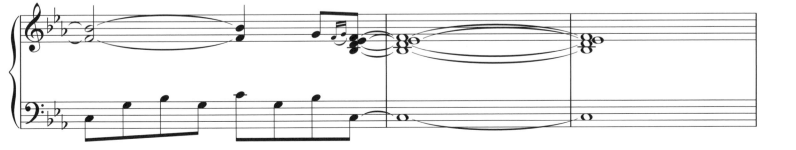

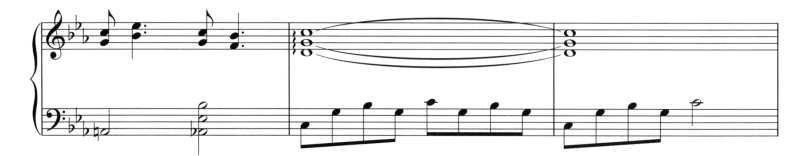

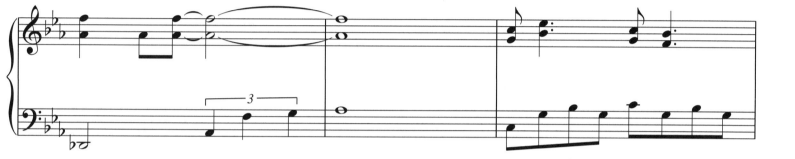

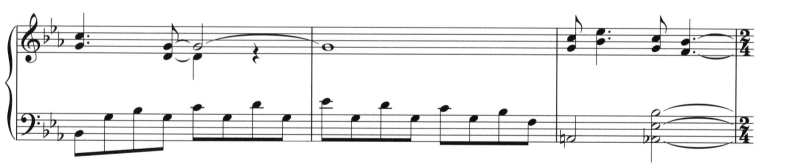

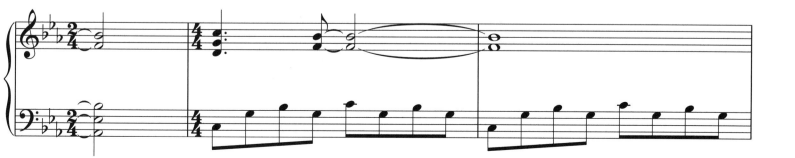

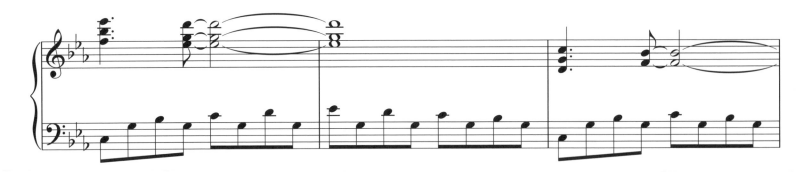

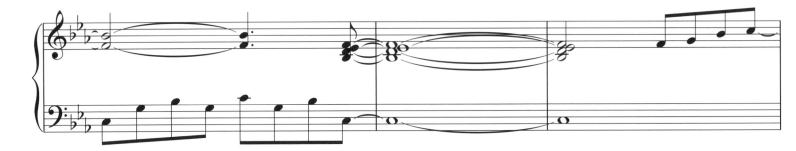

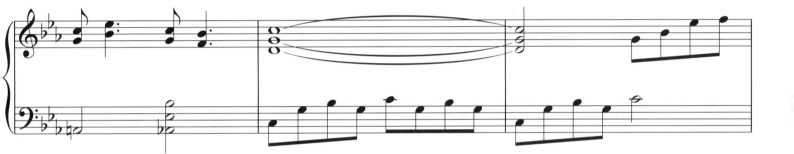

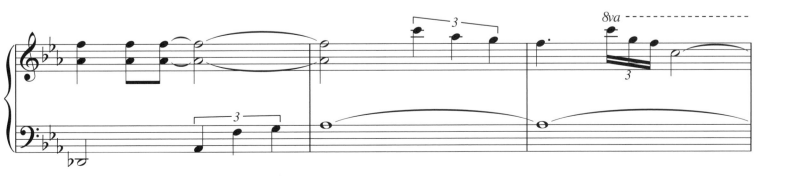

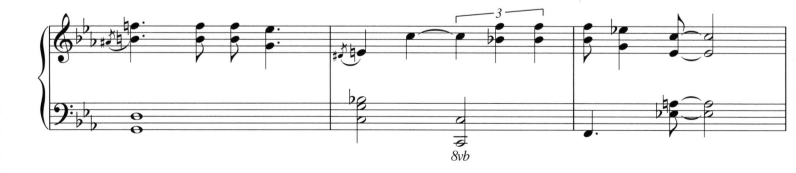

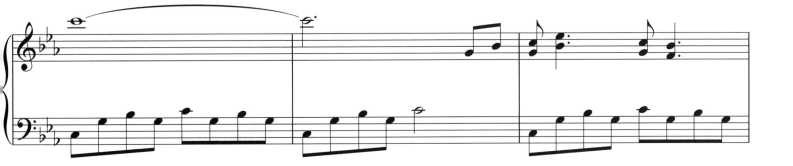

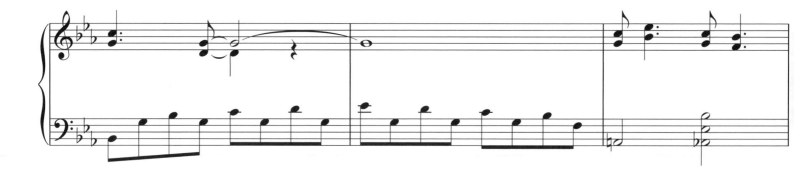

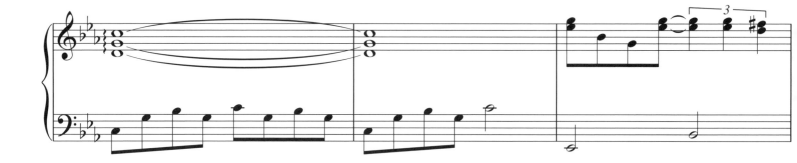

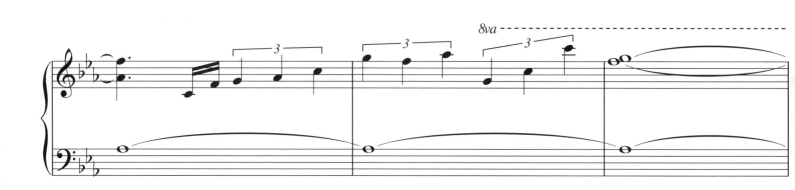

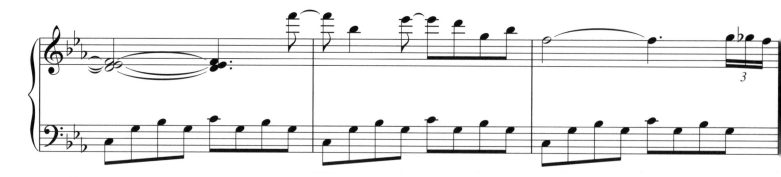

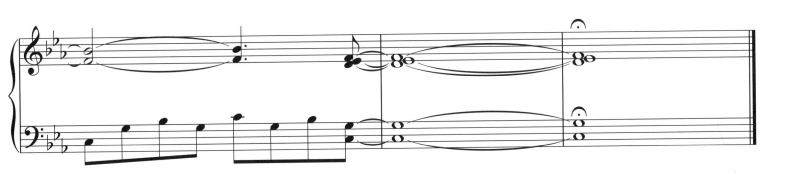

RAIN EIGHT DAYS A WEEK

Written by JOHN LENNON
and PAUL McCARTNEY

Moderately

Bring out melody

Pedal ad lib. throughout

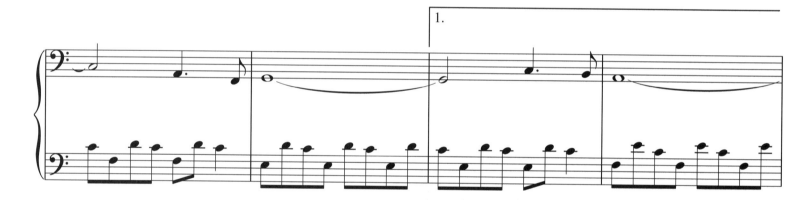

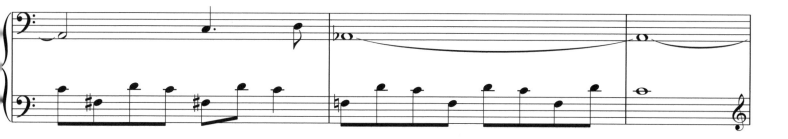

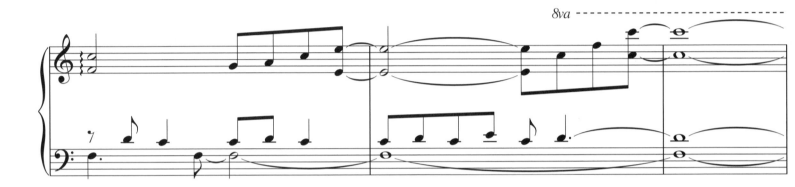

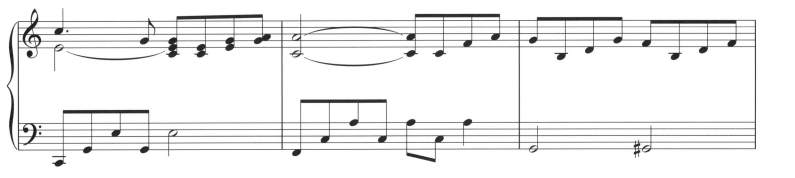

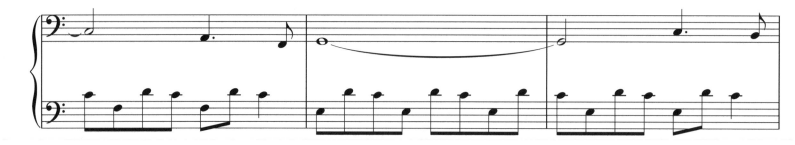

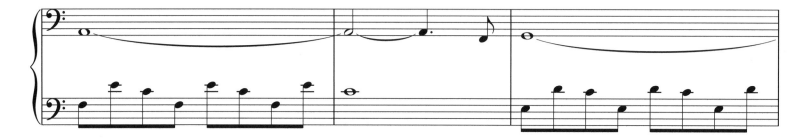

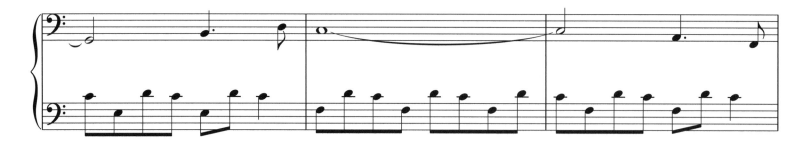

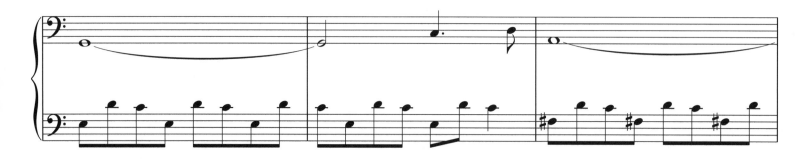

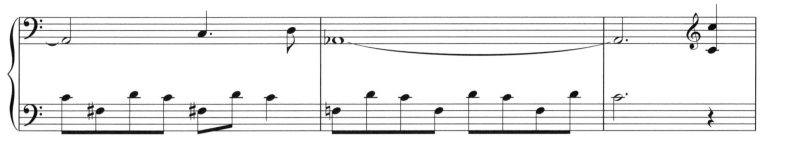

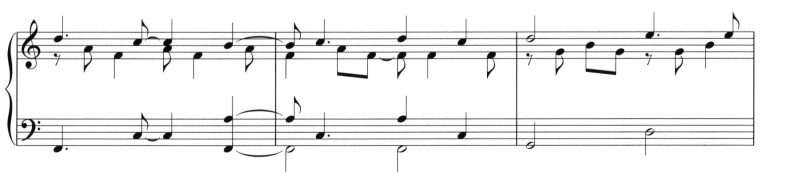

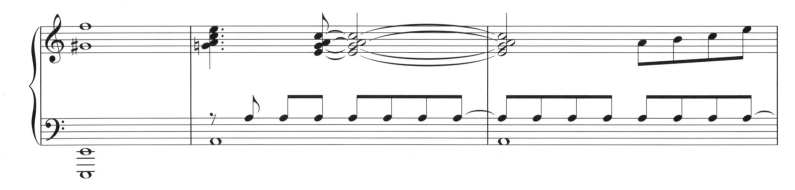

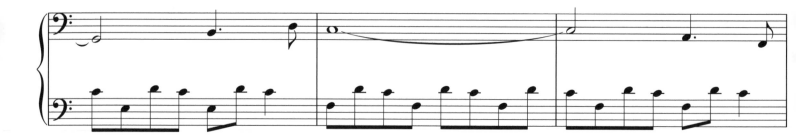

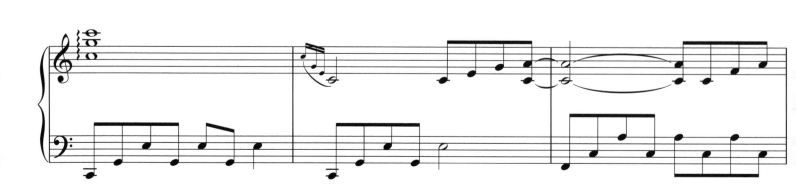

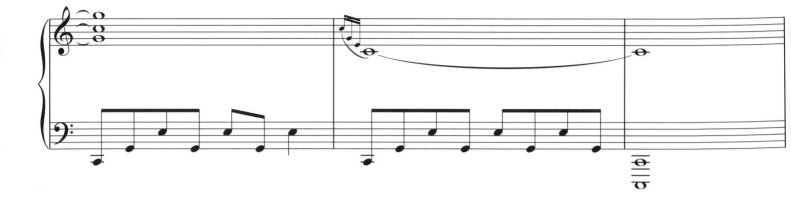

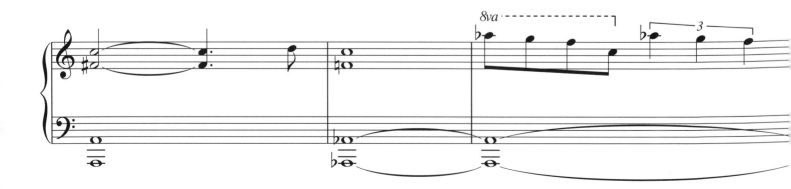

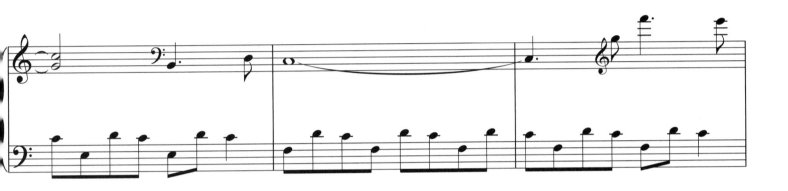

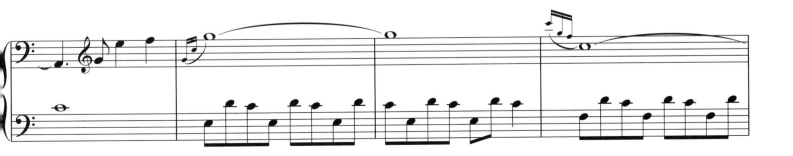

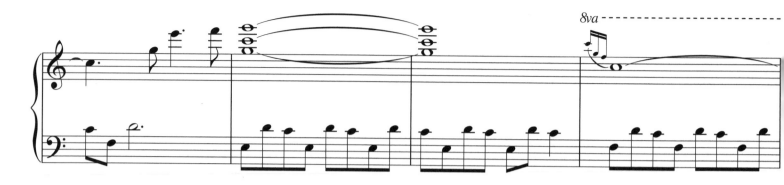

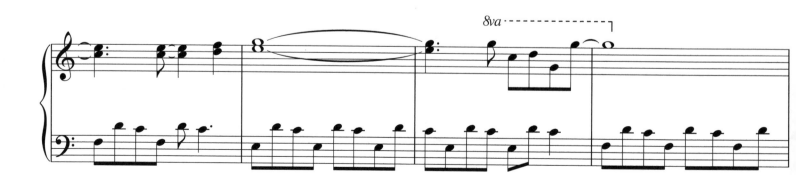

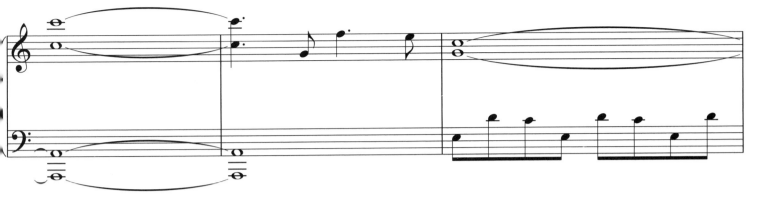

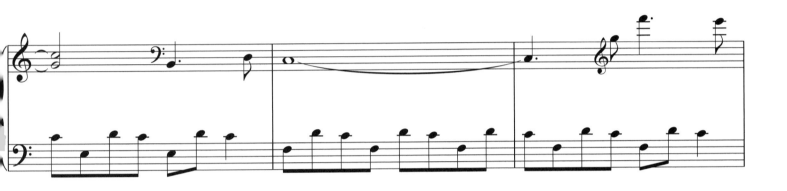

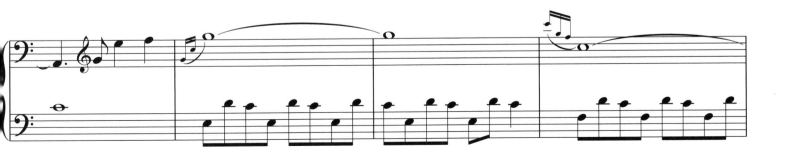

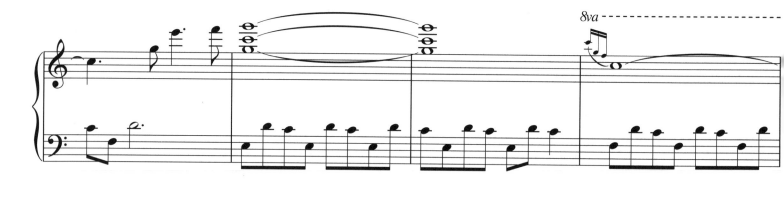

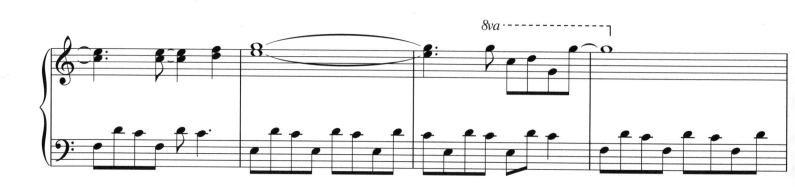

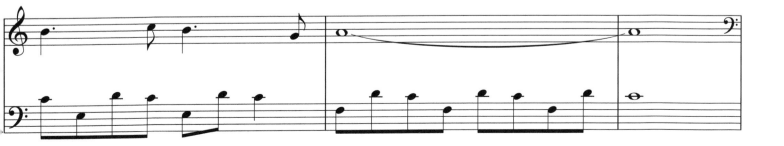

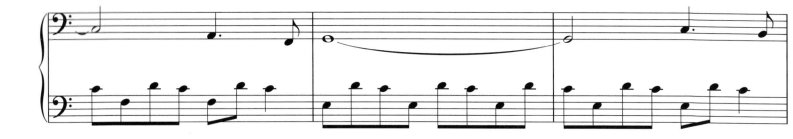

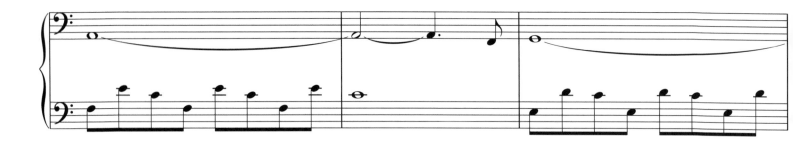

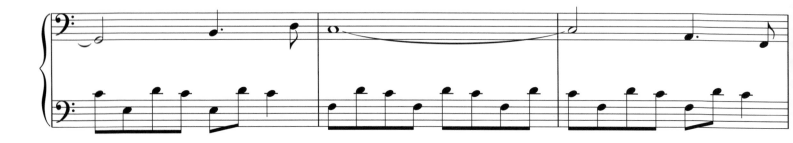

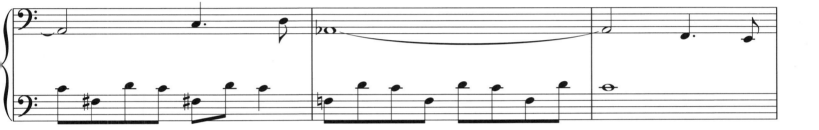

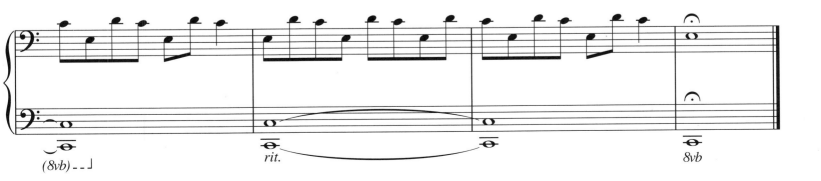

LOVELY RITA

The first five measures are taken from *Teatime for Rita*
(from the *Liverpool... Re-Imagining the Beatles* CD)

Words and Music by JOHN LENNON
and PAUL McCARTNEY

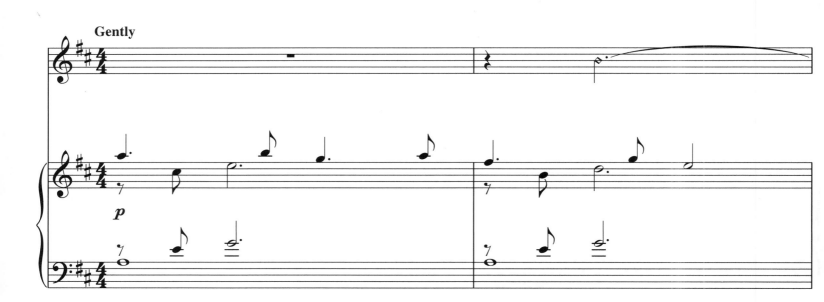

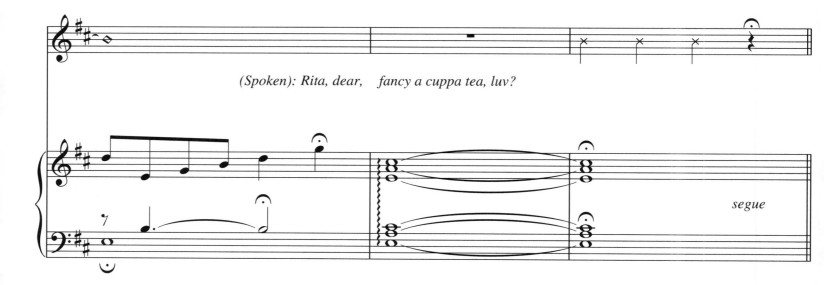

(Spoken): Rita, dear, fancy a cuppa tea, luv?

Moderately fast

mp

Pedal ad lib.

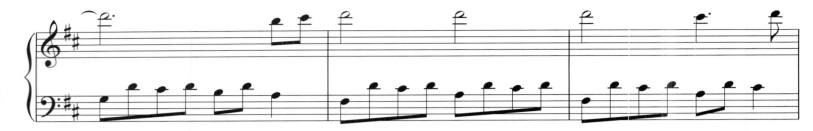

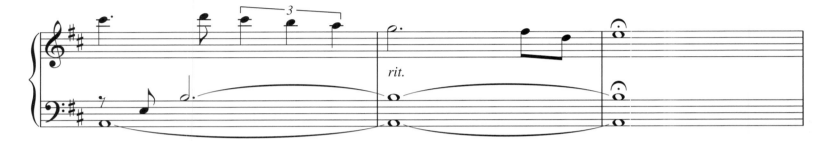

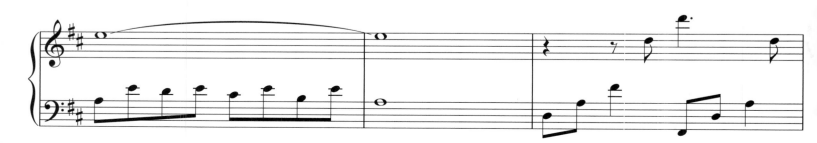

44

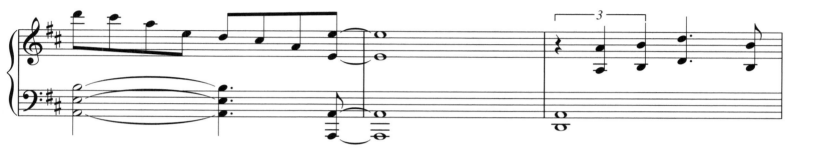

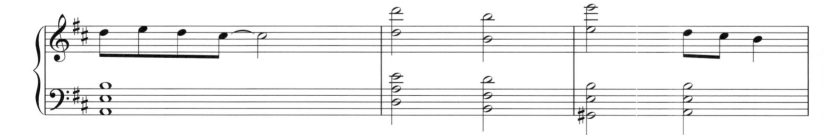

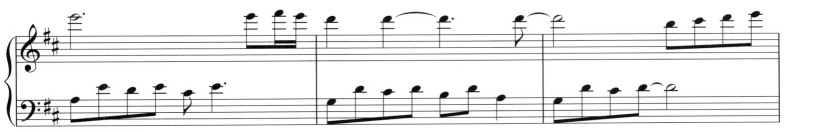

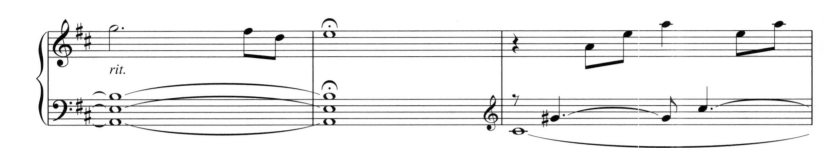

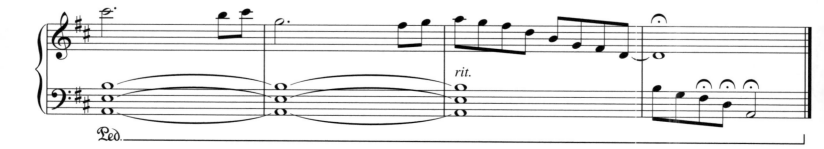

BECAUSE I'M ONLY SLEEPING

Written by JOHN LENNON
and PAUL McCARTNEY

Slowly, freely

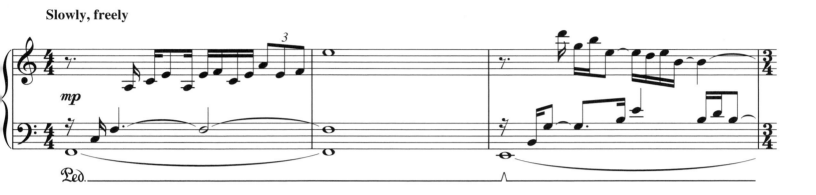

Moderately

Pedal ad lib. throughout

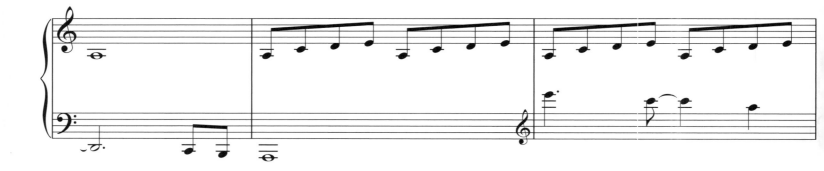

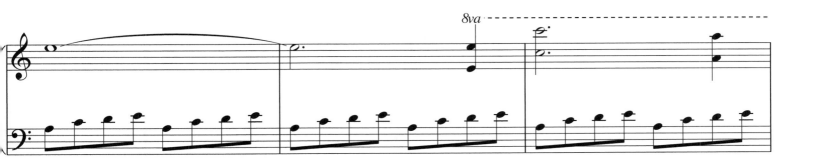

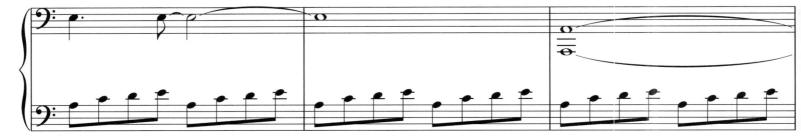

rit.

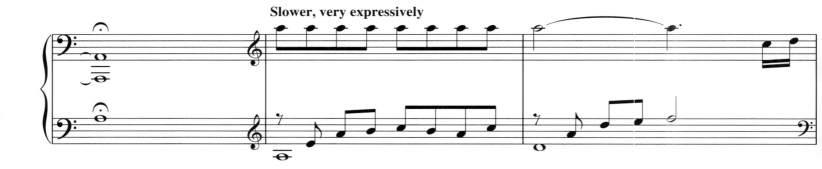

Slower, very expressively

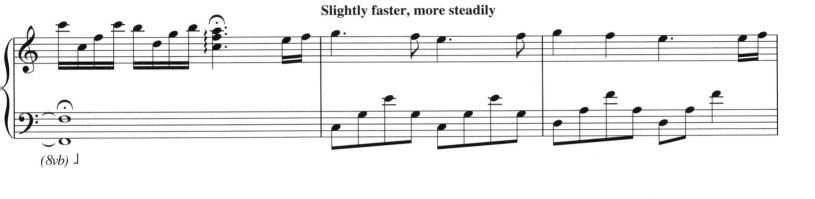

Slightly faster, more steadily

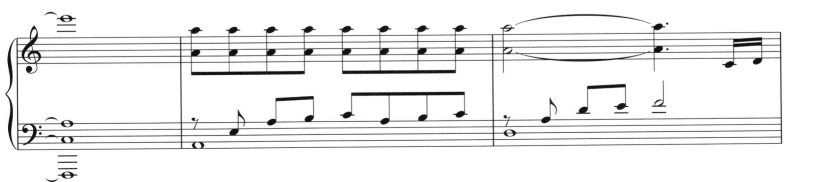

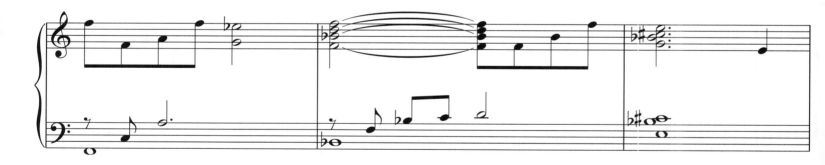

Steadily

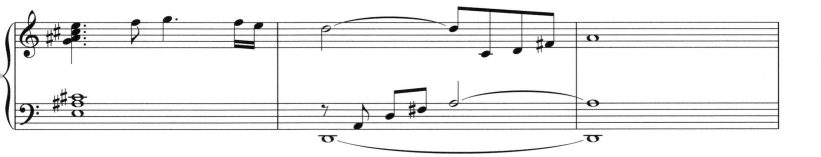

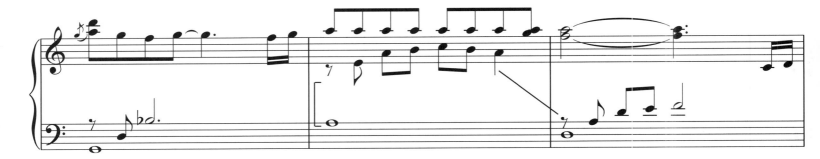

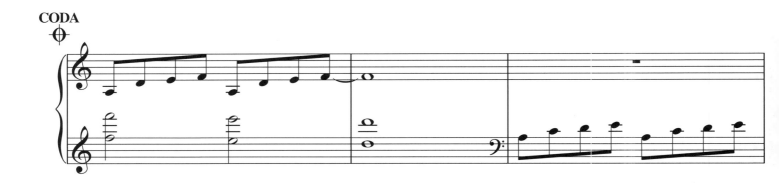

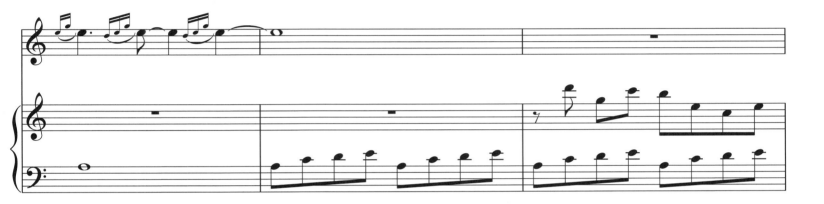

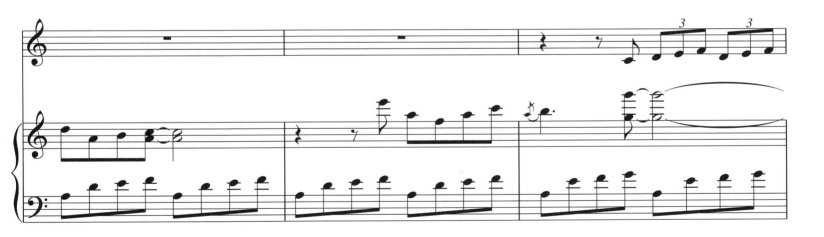

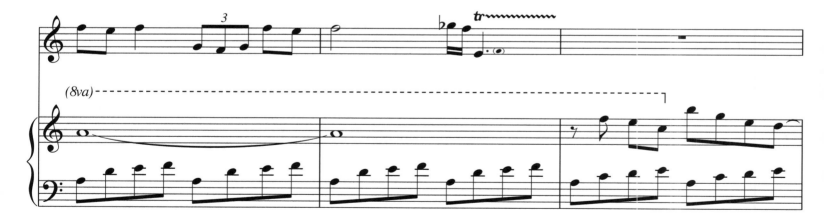

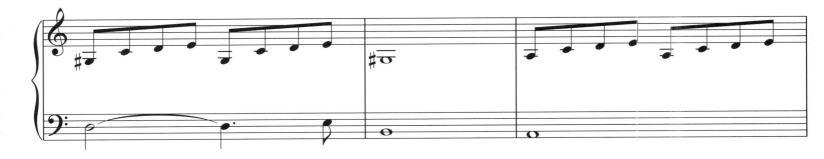

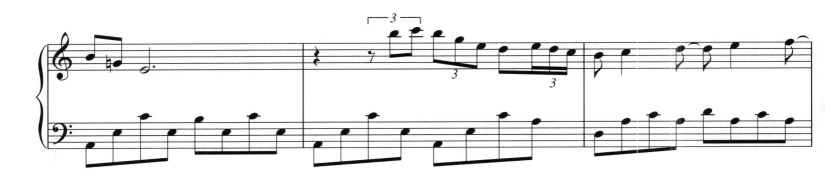

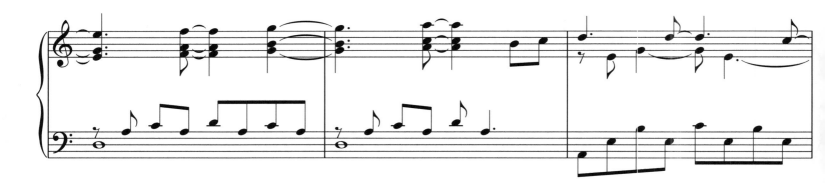

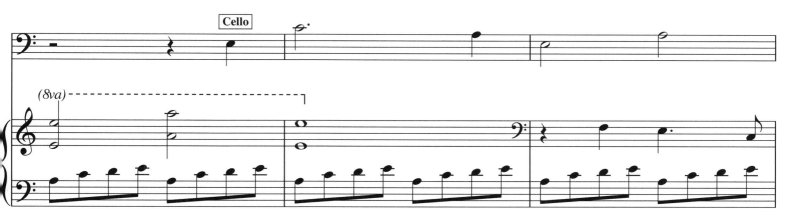

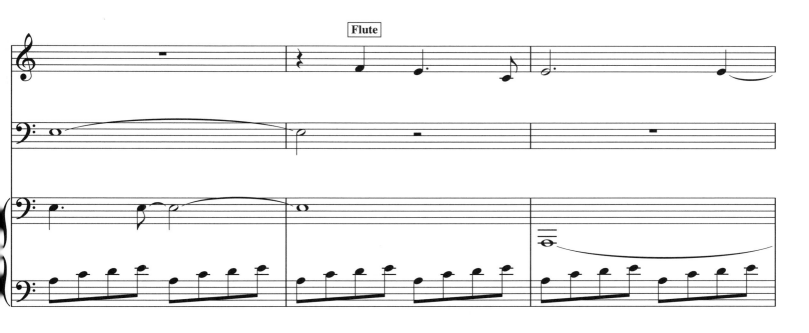

66

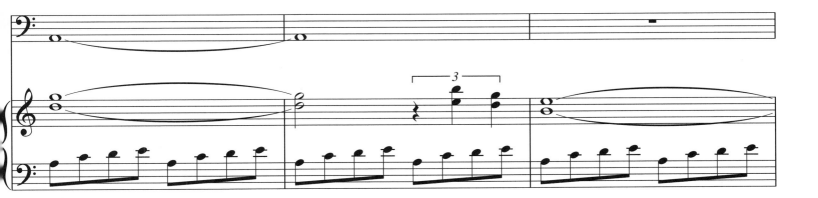

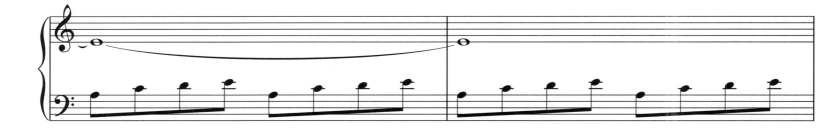

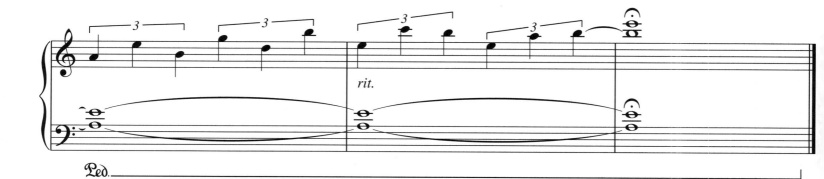

NORWEGIAN WOOD
(This Bird Has Flown)

Words and Music by JOHN LENNON
and PAUL McCARTNEY

Easily, in 1

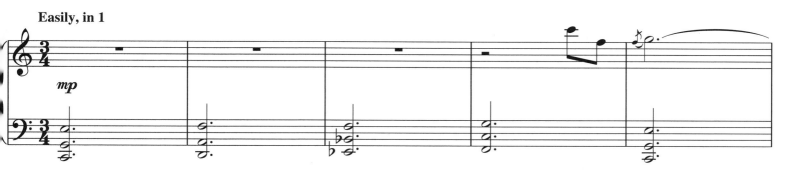

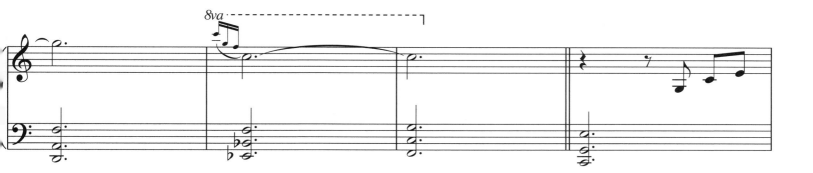

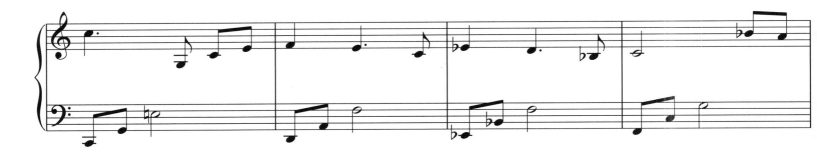

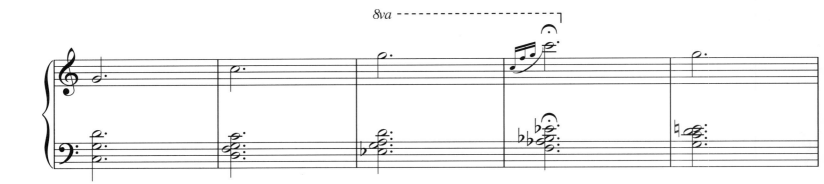

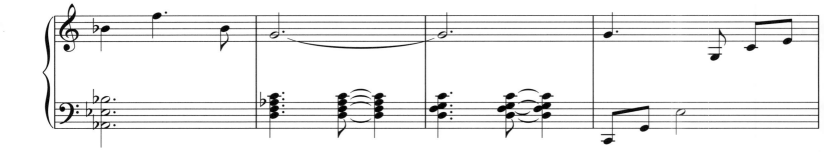

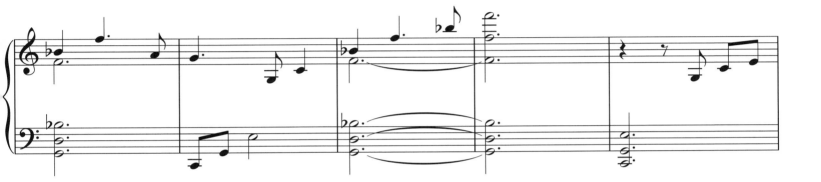

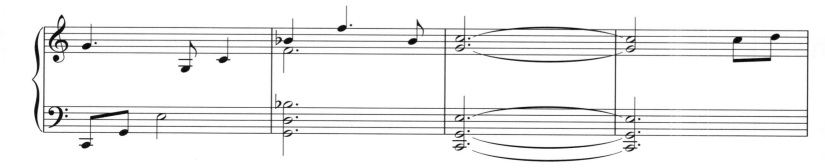

73

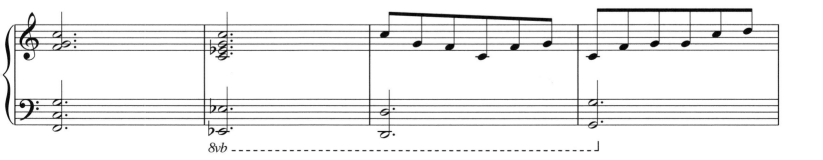

74

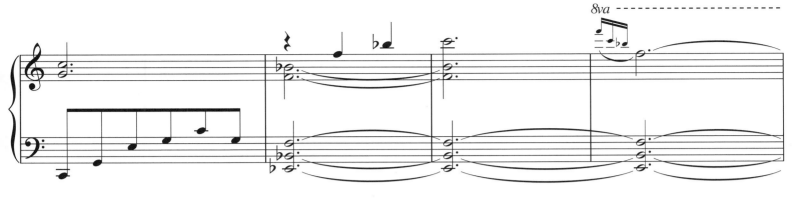

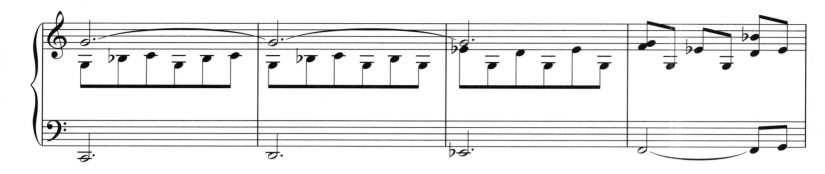

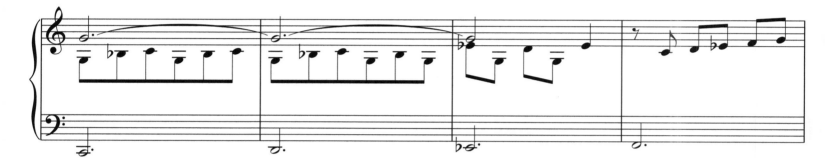

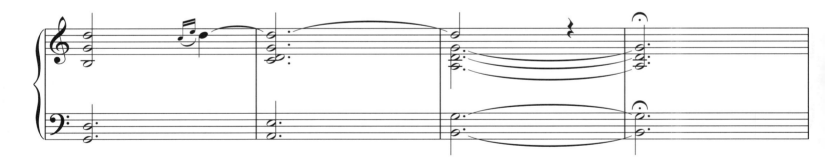

A tempo

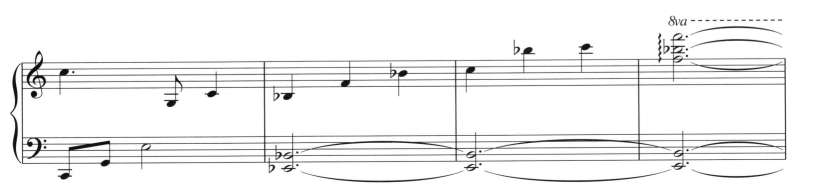

Freely

YES IT IS

Words and Music by JOHN LENNON
and PAUL McCARTNEY

Moderately

Pedal ad lib. throughout

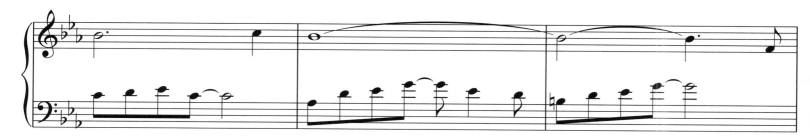

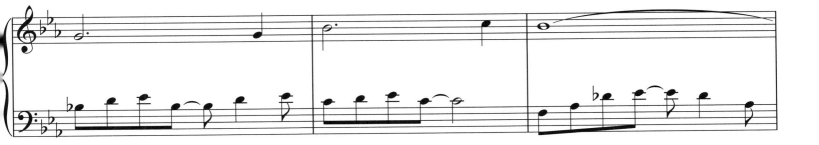

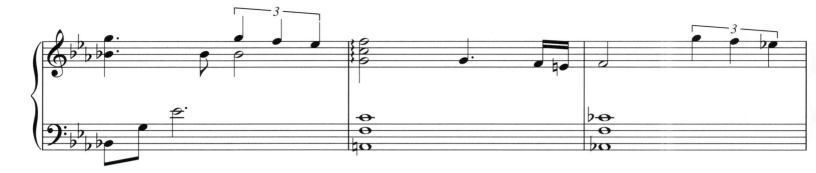

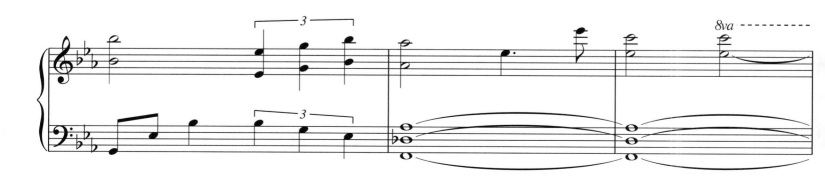

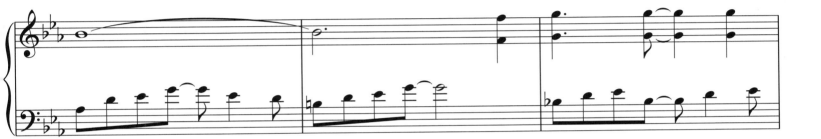

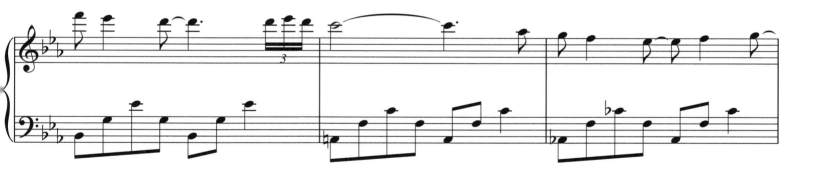

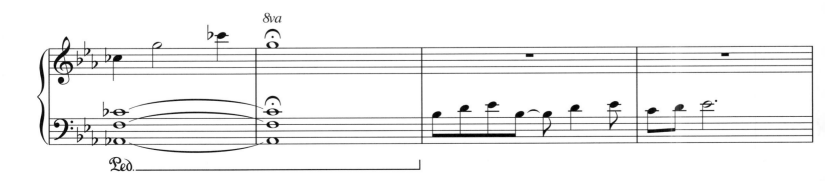

LONDON SKIES
A John Lennon Suite

Written by JOHN LENNON
and PAUL McCARTNEY

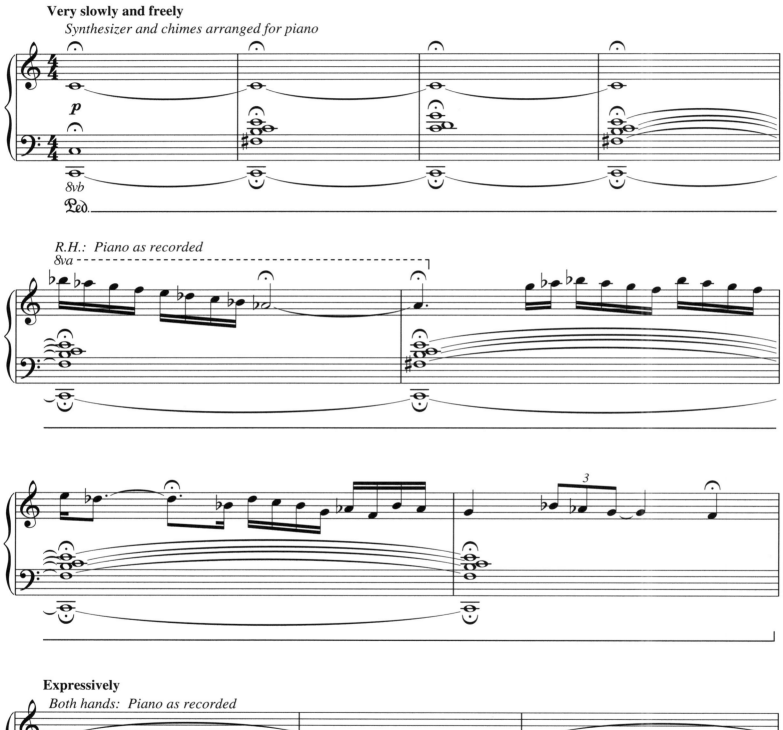

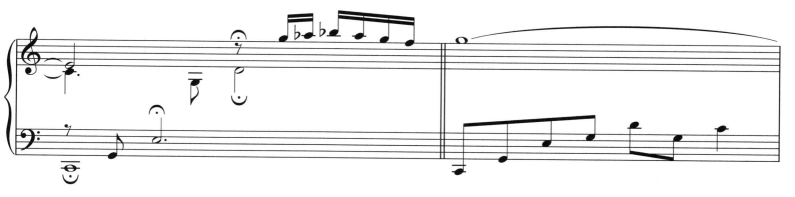

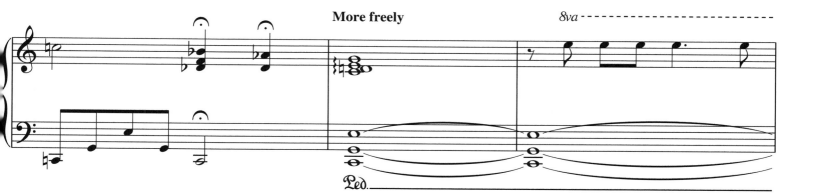

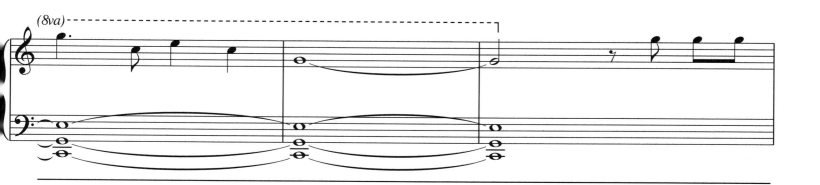

94

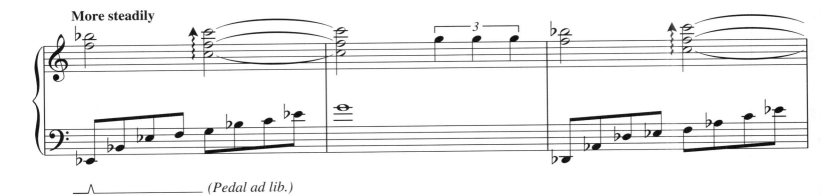

More steadily

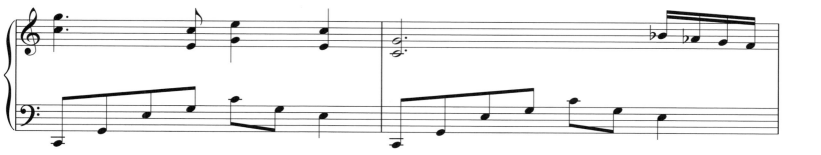

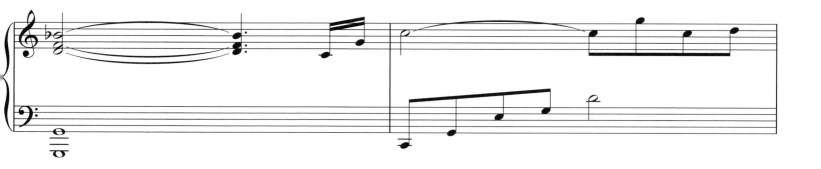

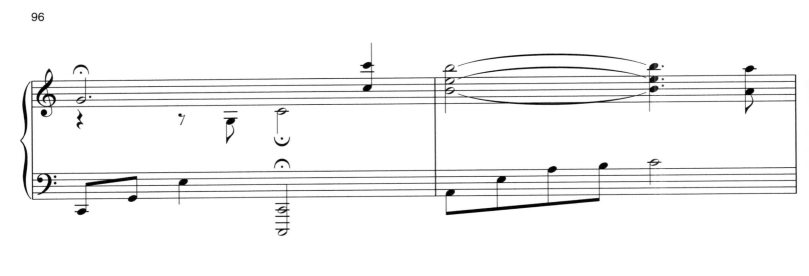

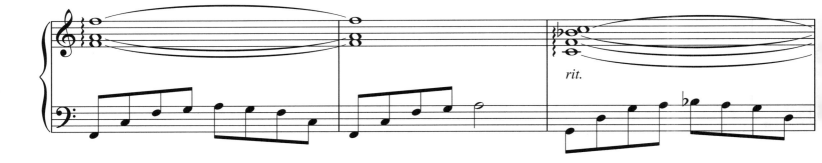

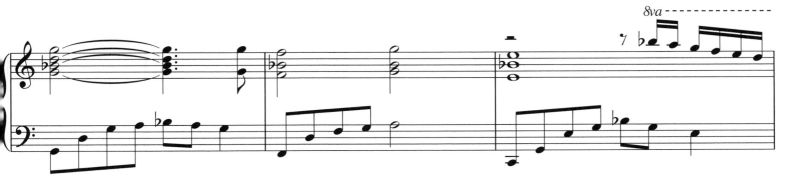

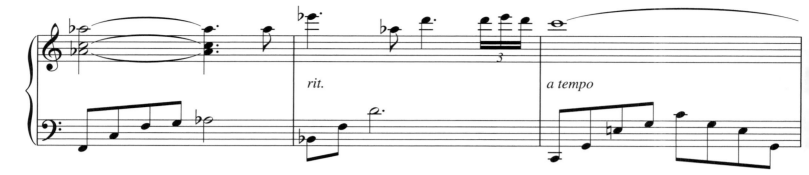

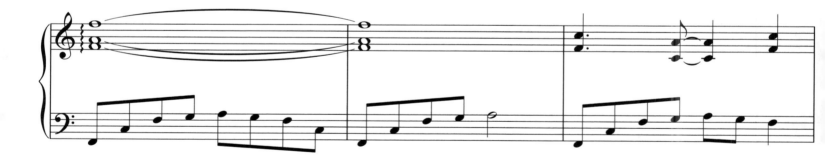

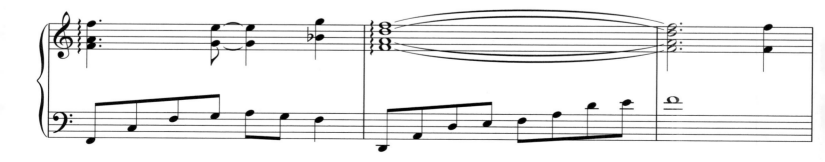

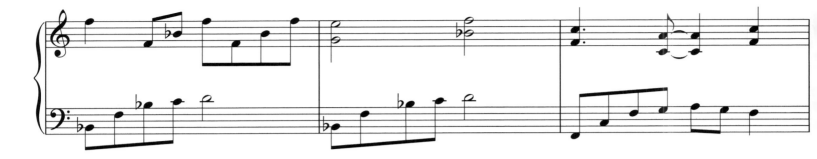

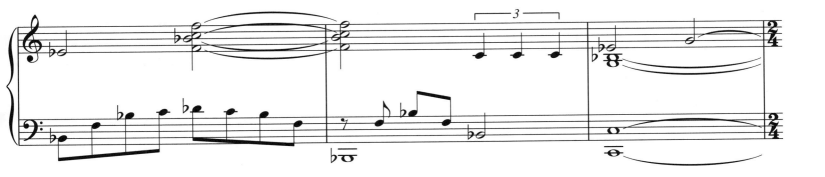

Slowly, freely

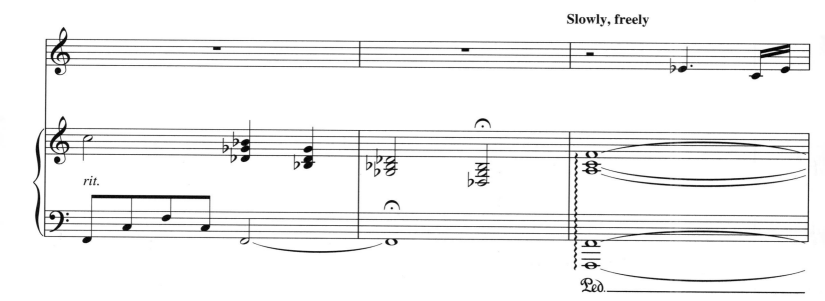

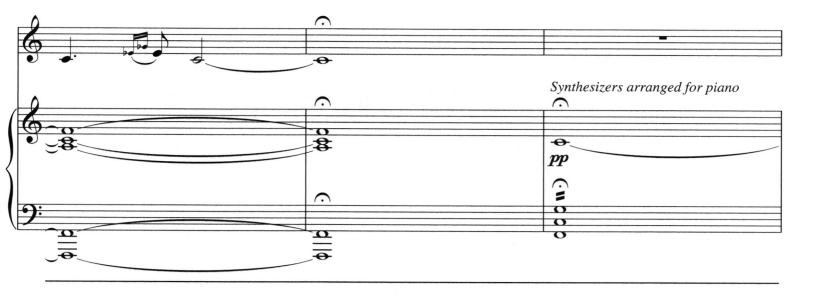

Synthesizers arranged for piano

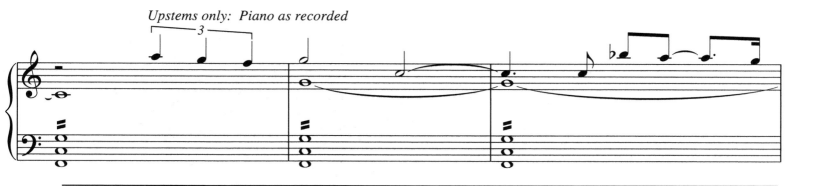

Upstems only: Piano as recorded

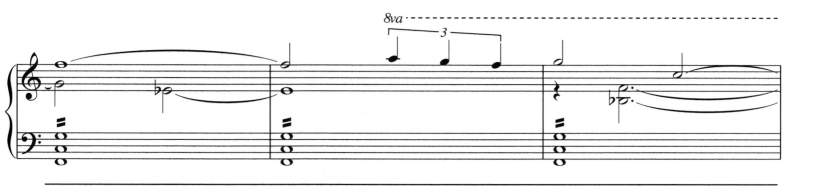

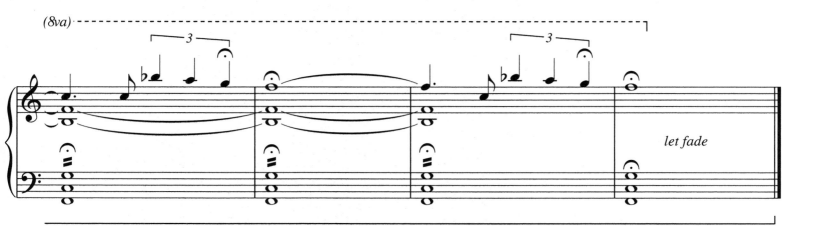

let fade